Celebrating Red Ribbon Week

Lesson Plans, Themes, Easy–to–Implement Ideas, Contest Ideas, Writing Prompts & Resources

This book has been made available through SAMHSA.

National
Recovery Month
Prevention Works · Treatment is Effective · People Recover
SEPTEMBER 2017

For help, feel free to contact the Center for Alcohol & Drug Services, Inc.

Written by Erainna Winnett, Ed.S.
Children's Book Author and Elementary School Counselor
counselingwithheart.com

Printed in the United States of America
ISBN-13: 978-0692202807
ISBN-10: 0692202803

Library of Congress Cataloging-in-Publication Data Winnett, Erainna
Celebrating Red Ribbon Week
Library of Congress Control Number: 2013978568

Table of Contents

Themes for the Week

It Is Super to Be Drug-Free	Wear a superhero cape to school because being drug-free is the super way to be! You can decorate your cape with wonderful reasons to be super healthy!
Put a Cap on Drugs!	Wear your favorite hat to school to let everyone know that you are helping put a cap on drugs!
Drugs Are Wacky!	Style your hair in a wacky fashion to show the world that drugs are wacky!
Better than Drugs Because	Dress for your future profession... because dream jobs are better than drugs!
Sock It to Drugs!	Sock it to drugs by wearing crazy socks to school!
Team Drug-Free!	Wear a sports jersey or uniform to sport your drug-free lifestyle. Everyone knows sports and drugs do NOT mix!
Red from Head to Toe!	Wear red in support of Red Ribbon Week and to show that you support being drug-free!
Rocking Red Ribbon Week!	Dress like a rock star to show why the drug-free lifestyle ROCKS!
Sticking with Drug-Free Friends!	Sport a strip of duct tape on your shirtsleeve to show the world that you stick with drug-free friends!

Twins Win Without Drugs!	Pick a partner and dress up as twins who win without drugs! Matching outfits can have a drug-free theme or simply be the same.
	Friends don't let friends do drugs!
Stomp Out Drug Use!	Wear your best stomping boots to show support for stomping out drug use!
Too Cool for Drugs!	Sport your favorite sunglasses to show everyone that you are too cool to use drugs!
Too Bright for Drugs!	Wear neon clothing to show the world that you are too bright for drugs!
Drug-Free Like Me!	Dress like your favorite drug-free role model.
	It can be a famous person or someone you admire.
Good Citizens Are Drug-Free!	Dress in patriotic clothing to show the world that you support being a good citizen by staying drug-free!
Smart People Don't Use Drugs!	Wear your favorite college T-shirt or hat, or dress like a college professor.
	Show everyone that you are too smart for drugs!
Drugs Are Spooky!	Wear a spooky costume to show the world that drugs are spooky, and we should scare them away! Do NOT include weapons, guts, or blood.
Drugs Send You the Wrong Way!	Wear your clothes backward to show that you will not be sent down the wrong path by using drugs!

Write Reasons to Be Drug-Free!	Write the right reason to stay away from drugs on a white T-shirt and wear it to school to show your friends why you choose to be drug-free!
Too Fancy to Use Drugs!	Wear your fanciest clothing to show the world that you are too fancy to try drugs.
Dreams, Not Drugs!	Wear your pajamas to school to show the world that you have big dreams!
Sporting the Drug-Free Lifestyle!	Wear exercise clothes to sport your drug-free look!
Spot Ways to Stay Free from Drugs!	Wear polka dots to show that you are spotting ways to stay drug-free for life!
Drugs Can't Rain on My Parade!	Wear a raincoat or carry an umbrella to show that drugs can't rain on you or your parade!
Tie Up Drugs!	Wear a tie to show that you support tying up drugs and living drug-free!

Contest Ideas

Door Decorating Contest	Decorate your classroom door with your very own theme for Red Ribbon Week. Winners can be selected for each grade level or school-wide.
Classroom Mural Contest	Each class can design a mural for Red Ribbon Week. This can serve as a kickoff event to RRW to determine which mural will hang in the multi-purpose room or in front of the school. Other prizes can also be designated.
Dances, Not Drugs	Students can participate in a "dance till you drop" contest to show their commitment to staying drug-free. They can also show their determination to have fun without drugs!
Too Cool for Drugs Talent Competition	Students can demonstrate their talents that make them too cool for drugs.
Poetry Contest	Students can enter their poems about living drug-free for submission to a poetry contest.
Essay Contest	Students can participate in an essay contest about why they choose to be drug-free.
Fine Arts Competition	Students can participate in a fine arts competition, entering pieces that are centered on the Red Ribbon Week theme.
Science Fair Competition	Students can enter science projects that center on health and the effects of drugs on the human body.

Cereal Box Contest	Students can decorate a cereal box featuring themes from Red Ribbon Week. Contest prizes can be awarded to the most creative, the most informative, and the most colorful.
Red Ribbon Week Obstacle Course	Students can compete as a class or individually in a race on an obstacle course. Winners get to wear large red ribbons indicating their placement.
Red Ribbon Scavenger Hunt	Students (divided into teams) can follow clues around campus to locate red ribbons. The team that collects the most WINS.
Pledge Drive	See which class can obtain the most signatures on a pledge to be drug-free.
Drugs Make You a Vegetable	Decorate a vegetable person and hold a contest for the silliest person.
Diorama Contest	Students can participate in a diorama competition that centers on drug-free living.
Red Ribbon Wreath Contest	Students can enter wreaths made out of red ribbon for a contest with a variety of prizes. These can include largest, silliest, and most creative use of ribbon.
Fact Bee	Students can compete in a true-or-false fact bee about drugs. (This is similar to a spelling bee, but they will instead be asked true-or-false questions about Red Ribbon Week themes.) This is a good way to finish off Red Ribbon Week.

Red Ribbon Week Penny Drive	Students can collect pennies for Red Ribbon Week, and each classroom can compete to see which collects the most. Money can be used to plan a pizza party for the winners (as well as to fund Red Ribbon Week next year). Make sure to discuss how much drugs cost a person and a community!
Slam Dunk Drugs	Students can participate in a slam dunk (or basketball shooting) contest to show that they are slamming drug use!

Easy-to-Implement Ideas

☐ Create a human red ribbon by having everyone dress in a red T-shirt. Stand on a field or in the parking lot in the form of a red ribbon and have a photograph taken.

☐ Have a poster parade. Students can create posters about Agent Enrique "Kiki" Camarena, Red Ribbon Week, or reasons to be drug-free. Then display the posters during the parade.

☐ Host a student art show in which students contribute pieces that are centered on Red Ribbon Week themes.

☐ Write letters to yourself about why you choose to be drug-free. Then save them to be mailed out one week prior to Red Ribbon Week next year. Letters can be addressed, stamped, and saved in the teacher's classroom.

☐ Class or small-group skits about staying drug-free can be performed for fellow classmates at a special assembly.

☐ Soar above drugs by flying kites with drug-free messages on them. Don't forget to tie a red ribbon onto each kite!

☐ Send a balloon to Agent Camarena thanking him for his service and sacrifice.

☐ Include your message inside of your balloon. Then release them as a class outdoors.

☐ Red Ribbon Scavenger Hunt: In groups or pairs, students can look for clues written on red ribbons tied all around the classroom or campus.

☐ Students can create a bookmark with a red ribbon and a drug-free message to exchange with their fellow classmates.

☐ Write off drugs by having students write with a red pen or colored pencil for the day.

☐ Have a red party in the classroom. Serve red foods such as tomatoes, strawberries, bell peppers, cherries, and red punch.

☐ Have students bring stuffed animals to school for a "Hugs Not Drugs" celebration.

☐ Drive out drugs by having students build cardboard boxcars to sit in drive-in style during a movie about drug-free awareness.

☐ Black out drugs by hosting a glow-in-the-dark dance party in the gym or cafeteria.

☐ Remember to be drug-free all year long by making red ribbon calendars to take home.

- Host a red ribbon pep rally. Distribute red ribbons for students to wear all week.

- Fly above drugs by making paper airplanes out of red construction paper.

- Have students fly their planes at a special recess. Make sure to write messages about staying drug-free on the airplanes.

- Celebrate hero citizens who keep our communities drug-free by writing a letter of gratitude and having the whole class sign it. Examples of honorees include police officers, principals, teachers, and coaches.

- Experimenting is for science, not drugs. Conduct a science experiment with the class about the effects of drugs on a person. For example, show students how drugs destroy lives by mixing baking soda and vinegar together in a 2-liter bottle for a sudsy spillover.

- Link up with good friends to keep drugs locked away. Create a human chain by linking arms with fellow classmates. If the whole school participates, that will be one long human chain! Make sure to snap a photograph for the yearbook.

- Bury a red ribbon-themed time capsule for a future class to find. Include reasons you choose to stay drug-free.

- Since drugs create so many obstacles, have students run an obstacle course!

- Remind them that there is a way around, over, or through every challenge.

- Write a representative, senator, or congressperson. Provide students with research about drug use in their community. Then ask them to write a letter to their political representatives about the situation. Include a proposed solution to the problem.

- Remember that drugs are trash by having a clean-up day for the school or campus. Students can sort recyclables, pick up trash, and clean up their campus to see how much better things are without all the trash around.

- Celebrate saving for the good life by having students bring in spare change.

- Collect it in a large jar. Discuss with students the financial impacts of using drugs. Then donate the collected change to a charity of students' choosing. Make sure to contrast helping the community with money versus wasting it on drugs.

Red Ribbons Show We Care

Dear Parents,

Next week our school will celebrate Red Ribbon Week. Many students across the nation have Red Ribbon Week at their school. They wear red ribbons. They dress in silly clothes. They wear red T-shirts. They learn about living drug-free. Many students want to know why they wear red ribbons during this week.

In 1985, a brave officer gave his life to save people from drugs. To support this hero, people wore red ribbons. They believed in his cause. They wanted to show that they supported living drug-free. This group of people shared their idea with the First Lady, Nancy Reagan. Mrs. Reagan also cared a lot about drug-free living. She wore a red ribbon, too.

Schools started supporting the red ribbon cause. They started wearing them for one week in October and November. Schools across the country joined in by wearing red ribbons. Students learned about being drug-free from an early age. They learned that drugs are bad. They learned why drugs are dangerous. Parent Teacher Organizations helped organize weeks to wear red ribbons.

Soon, a group of people who supported families wanted to help. They founded National Red Ribbon Week. Mrs. Reagan asked lawmakers to help. They decided that Red Ribbon Week was a great idea, and they wore them, too. The idea grew into a national celebration. Every year, more than 80 million people celebrate Red Ribbon Week.

Red Ribbon Week teaches students about living drug-free. Students learn why drugs are dangerous. They learn how to say no to drugs. They learn how to make good choices to stay away from drugs. There are many reasons to be drug-free. Red Ribbon Week is a time to remember those reasons together. We wear red ribbons to show that we care about drug-free living. Please join us and support your child and their school next week as we, too, learn to live drug-free.

Sincerely,

The Story Behind Red Ribbon

Why Do We Wear Red Ribbons?

Many students across the nation observe Red Ribbon Week in their schools and communities. During Red Ribbon Week, they wear silly outfits, red ribbons, and red T-shirts. All of these things are meant to teach students about drugs. They learn why drugs are dangerous and should be avoided. They learn how to live a drug-free lifestyle. They learn how to help their friends and families make good choices and stay away from drugs. Many students wonder what red ribbons have to do with learning about living a drug-free lifestyle.

In 1985, a very brave drug enforcement officer gave his life to save people from the dangers of drugs. This officer was very well-respected. People who knew him wanted to support his life work and cause. They wanted people to know he had given his life to save people from drugs. To show their support, they wore red ribbons with his name on them. The red ribbons also showed support for living a drug-free lifestyle. Soon, this same group of people shared their idea with the First Lady, Nancy Reagan. (The First Lady is the president's wife.) Mrs. Reagan worked very hard to fight against drugs, just like the brave officer. She supported the group's cause by wearing red ribbons along with them.

Everyone in the country saw Mrs. Reagan's red ribbon because she was on television. Her picture was often in newspapers. Many people respected her reasons for wearing a red ribbon. Parents and teachers thought it would be a wonderful idea to wear red ribbons in their schools. They thought it was a good way to teach students about drugs. They wanted to keep drugs out of their schools and away from their kids. They started wearing red ribbons in October and November of each year. Mrs. Reagan and the president supported the schools wearing red ribbons.

As the ribbons spread across the country, others took notice. The National Family Partnership, with the help of Mrs. Reagan, founded National Red Ribbon Week in 1988. They even took Red Ribbon Week all the way to the nation's capital, Washington, D.C. They told Congress about Red Ribbon Week, and soon even the lawmakers wore red ribbons! Each year, more and more people participated in Red Ribbon Week. Communities began to realize that standing against drugs was important. Teaching kids about drugs was also very important. Each time a person pinned on a red ribbon or tied one to their school fence, they told the world they were saying "No!" to drugs. They told the world that they honored the brave drug enforcement officer.

Today, more than 80 million people participate in Red Ribbon Week across the country. Every fall, schools and communities organize events to show their support of drug-free living. These events have contests, silly dress- up days, and lots of red ribbons. Children learn ways to say no to drugs, even if there is peer pressure. Citizens remember the hero who helped fight off drugs. Students take pledges to stay drug-free for life. Communities come together to stand against drugs and to promote a drug-free lifestyle. Red Ribbon Week represents the reasons that drugs are not safe for people. It represents the reasons that citizens wish to stay drug-free. Red ribbons show the world how many people stand against drugs.

Directions: Draw a ribbon below, write your reasons to be drug-free, and then color the ribbon red.

Grades K–1

Red Ribbon Week Writing Prompts

Writing prompts may need to vary for pre-writers. Kindergarteners might need to have a picture prompt in addition to, or instead of, a writing prompt. These are given below the writing prompts.

1) Malcom's older brother smelled funny. His clothes smelled like smoke. Malcom did not like the smoky smell. He used to like wearing his brother's big sweater. Now it smelled too smoky. Malcom loved his brother very much. He decided to talk to his brother about the funny smell.

   a) How do you think Malcom's brother answered him?

   b) Do you think Malcom was right to ask his brother about the funny smell?

Option for pre-writing students: Malcom has a brother who started smelling smoky. Draw a picture of Malcom with his brother when he smells good and a picture when he smells smoky.

2) Sometimes we take medicine when we are sick. It can help us feel better. It can keep us well. Medicine must be taken carefully. Most families have rules about medicine. Children should never take medicine without an adult. What are some of your family's rules about medicine?

Option for pre-writing students: Draw a picture of a safe way to take medicine when you need it.

3) Drugs are bad for our bodies. They can make us sick. It is important to stay healthy. There are many ways to stay healthy instead of sick. Never taking drugs is one way. What are some other ways you can live a healthy life?

Option for pre-writing students: Draw a picture that tells how you stay healthy.

Red Ribbon Week

_____

_____

_____

_____

Grades 2–3

Red Ribbon Week Writing Prompts

1) There are a lot of reasons for me to stay away from drugs. Some people use drugs because they think they will feel good. I don't need drugs to feel good. There are many ways that I can feel good. The thing I do that makes me feel happiest is...

2) My future matters to me. I have big plans. My plans do not include drugs. Drugs will only get in the way of my success. Instead of drugs, I am going to do great things. When I grow up, I am going to be...

3) My teacher said that some kids try drugs. Sometimes, their friends try them and want to share. Real friends do not share drugs. Good friends stay away from drugs. I want to be a good friend. I also want to choose good friends. My friends and I can be good to each other by staying away from drugs. One way we can do this is to...

Red Ribbon Week

Grades 4–6

Red Ribbon Week Writing Prompts

Read the story starter below and then write your own ending.

1) Jamie was new to Annie's school. The girls were quick to become friends. They had the same backpack and had the same favorite color. Their birthdays were even close together. One day, Jamie asked Annie to meet at the park to play after school. When Annie got to the park, Jamie gave her a hug. Then she showed her a bottle of small white pills. Jamie offered one of the pills to Annie. Annie knew she should not take them, but Jamie said they would have even more fun playing if they did. She said they were like candy. Annie decided that she should not take the pill. She also did not want to hurt her friend's feelings. Annie decided that honesty was the best policy. She told Jamie about Red Ribbon Week at school...

2) Some people try drugs because they think it will make them "fit in." Smart kids know that there are many ways to "fit in" with their peers. They know that they can make friends by...

3) Write three paragraphs about why you choose to stay drug-free. Include at least three reasons and three goals you have to help keep you successful.

Red Ribbon Week

_____

_____

_____

_____

_____

_____

_____

_____

_____

_____

_____

_____

_____

_____

_____

_____

Using the words Drug Free, write an acrostic poem that tells all of the wonderful things about you!

D

R

U

G

F

R

E

E

Grades K–1

Red Ribbon Week Lesson Plans

Lesson Plan: Popsicle Stick Puppets Stay Drug-Free

This lesson will take approximately 30–45 minutes to implement.

Objective: Students will demonstrate understanding that smoking and drugs are harmful to health.

Content Standard: *Recognize that tobacco smoke is harmful to health and should be avoided.*

Method and Materials: Discussion, art, and storytelling. Popsicle sticks, markers, glue, yarn.

Anticipatory Set: Tell students the following story about the dangers of tobacco smoke.

Matt and the Smoky Smell

Matt and his dad went to the hospital to visit his grandfather. While they were walking into the hospital, a man was outside smoking a cigarette. He blew out a big puff of smoke right when Matt walked by him. Matt coughed. His eyes watered.

"Dad, that smoke sure is yucky. It hurts my eyes and my throat," Matt told his father. Matt's father gripped his hand and patted his back. Matt didn't like the smelly smoke. He could smell it all the way into the elevator. It seemed to cling to his nostrils. Matt closed his eyes, stuck out his tongue, and shook his head to get rid of the smell.

"Smoking sure is yucky, Son. It also makes you very sick. Your grandfather smoked cigarettes for many years. They made him very sick. That's why he's in the hospital today."

Matt knew his grandfather liked to smoke. Even though he loved his grandfather very much, he didn't like the smoky smell. He especially didn't like to hear that his grandfather was sick because of smoking. He didn't know that smoking could make someone sick. Matt decided then and there that he would never, ever try smoking a cigarette.

Introduction: Ask students discussion questions about the story.

1) Has anyone ever smelled cigarette smoke?

2) Has anyone ever known someone who got sick from smoking?

3) Why did Matt decide that he would never, ever try smoking cigarettes?

Instruction – Input and Modeling: Show students a finished Popsicle stick puppet. You can introduce the puppet as Matt from the story. "Matt" will tell the students the following facts about tobacco smoke.

WORDS TO KNOW:

Secondhand smoke: smoke that is blown near nonsmokers and can make them sick

Cancer: a disease that is sometimes caused by smoking

Lungs: the organs that are responsible for breathing

1) A single cigarette has more than 4,800 chemicals, and 70 of those chemicals cause cancer.

2) Secondhand smoke contains over 7,000 chemicals, including 70 cancer- causing chemicals.

3) Smoking causes a variety of lung diseases.

4) Smoking kills 1 in 5 people in the United States every year.

Check for Understanding: "Matt" will ask students how many chemicals are found in a cigarette, how many people are killed from smoking, and how many chemicals cause cancer. Ask students to respond chorally.

Guided Practice: Pass out materials to make puppets. Students will make their own Popsicle stick puppet who will advocate for no smoking. Students will require step-by-step instructions.

1) Glue yarn to the top of the stick for hair.

2) Draw a face on the stick.

3) Cut out strips of paper to make clothes for the puppet.

Independent Practice: Students will share their puppets with the class or with a small group. Each student will recite one fact related to smoking with his or her puppet.

Extension Activities

1) Poster: Students will create a poster explaining what they have learned about the difference between drugs and medicine. These can be included in the Red Ribbon Week poster contest. (Complete on construction paper.)

2) Rules for Medicine: Students will determine safe rules for medicine and make a rule chart for their homes. Students should share these rule charts with their families and then share with the class how their families responded to the rule charts.

3) Love Our Lungs: Students will participate in activities that celebrate lung capacity. Outdoors, students can be timed running 200-yard dash races. They can also compete in screaming "Say no to drugs!" at the top of their lungs. Connect this activity to the dangers of smoking and the damage it does to the lungs. Pass out the "Color My Lungs!" worksheet for students to color healthy lungs and unhealthy lungs.

Color My Lungs!

Color one set of lungs a healthy pink and the other set an unhealthy black. Which set would you rather have in your body?

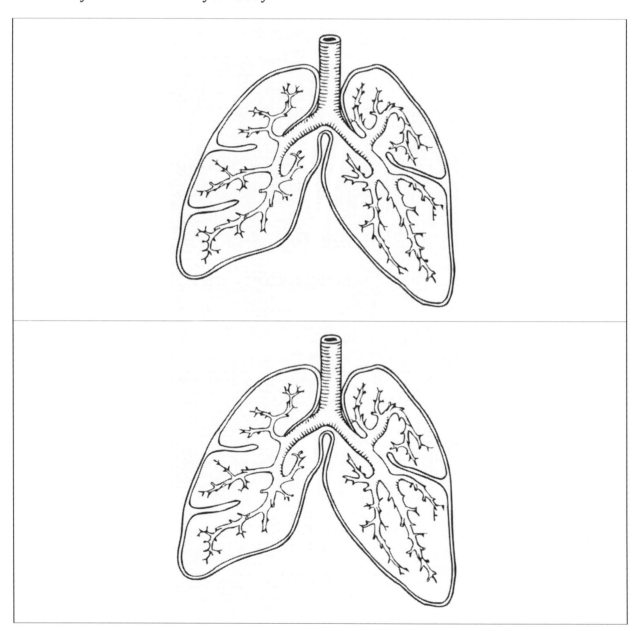

Red Ribbon Week Lesson Plans
Grades 2–3

Lesson Plan: Is It Safe or Dangerous?

This lesson should require approximately 30 minutes for instruction and practice. Extension activities might require more time or can be kept on hand for early finishers.

Objective: Students will demonstrate understanding of the dangers of tasting, swallowing, sniffing, or otherwise examining an unknown substance.

Content Standard: *Explain why it is dangerous to taste, swallow, sniff, or play with unknown substances.*

Method and Materials: Discussion and student-made graphic organizers. Poster paper, markers, and premade sample of activity.

- Premade sample directions: Fold a piece of poster paper into thirds.
  Using the markers, outline three columns. Draw a line to divide each column in half. Label each top column accordingly:

  - When something is definitely unsafe, I... (Share good ways to handle what to do when you find an unsafe substance.)

    - Underneath this column, draw a list of things that are definitely unsafe.

  - When something might be unsafe, I...(Share good ways to handle what to do when you find a substance that may be unsafe.)

    - Underneath this column, draw a list of things that might be unsafe.

  - When something is almost certainly safe, I...(Share good ways to handle what to do when you find a substance that is probably safe.)

    - Underneath this column, draw a list of things that are almost certainly safe.

Your premade sample will look like this:

Review: Ask students to briefly discuss the following questions with a share partner. Allow a few students to share their answers with the class.

1) Are there some plants that are unsafe to touch?

2) Are there some chemicals that could be unsafe to smell?

3) How do you know if a substance is unsafe or not?

4) How can you tell if a plant is dangerous?

Anticipatory Set: Share the following story with the class.

In November 2012, a woman in San Francisco picked mushrooms out of her backyard and added them to a homemade soup. She had never seen the mushrooms before, but she figured they were safe since they looked similar to ones she had eaten. The woman served the soup to two of her family members and ate some of it herself. Hours after eating the mushrooms, the two family members died, and she became violently ill. As it turned out, the mushrooms were extremely poisonous. The woman did not realize this before she served them.

Introduction: Discuss with the class the consequences of guessing incorrectly about whether a plant is safe or dangerous. Then ask the class for examples of other substances that can be safe or dangerous, such as medicine or household chemicals. Ask the following discussion questions:

1) Are there other things that might look safe but could really be dangerous?

2) List examples on the board of things that might be unsafe.

3) Why do we have rules about medicine and household cleaners?

   a) *List on the board some of the rules that students have at home.*

4) What should you do if you encounter a substance and you are not sure if it is safe or not?

Check for Understanding: Ask students a few thumbs-up or thumbs-down questions to make sure they are on target to understanding the lesson.

1) When you find a glass of liquid and don't know what is in it, you should taste it.

   (Wait for choral response NO!)

2) When you find a new flower growing in the woods, it is okay to smell it after you ask an adult if it is okay.

   (Wait for choral response YES!)

Guided Practice: Direct students to fold the poster paper and create columns as written in the sample. As a class, discuss good ways to handle each situation. Then discuss substances or plants that might fall into each category.

Independent Practice: Students will create their own poster charts and then share them with classmates.

Lesson Plan: Who Has the Right Answers?

This lesson should require approximately 30 minutes for instruction and practice. Extension activities might require more time or can be kept on hand for early finishers.

Objective: Students will demonstrate the ability to distinguish credible and safe sources of information about drugs and alcohol.

Content Standard: *Identify parents, guardians, and trusted adults who can provide accurate information and guidance regarding medicines.*

Method and Materials: Discussion and chart project. Paper and pen or pencil and handouts.

Review: Ask students to briefly discuss the following questions with a share partner. Allow a few students to share their answers with the class.

1) Who can you trust for truthful and accurate information?

2) Which adults can you trust to answer questions about drugs and alcohol?

3) How do you know when someone is telling the truth?

4) If you wanted to know something about drugs or alcohol, who would you ask?

Anticipatory Set: Read the following "facts" to the class and ask them to decide which are true and which are false. When they have made their guesses, reveal which facts are true and which are false.

1) Elephants carry their young for almost two years before giving birth. (true)

2) You could produce enough energy to heat a cup of water if you yelled for 8 years and 7.1 months. (true)

3) Peanut butter can explode when added to baking soda. (false)

4) Cows will not walk downstairs. (true)

5) People can use photosynthesis to absorb energy. (false)

6) Some people can breathe underwater. (false)

7) Abraham Lincoln invented the Internet. (false)

8) Eating fruits and vegetables is a good way to stay healthy and grow strong. (true)

9) Koalas have very similar fingerprints to humans. (true)

10) Ducks are capable of laying chicken eggs. (false)

Introduction: Some of the facts we read above were true and others were false. False information can sometimes be easy to believe, especially if it is about something we know little about. Drugs and alcohol can be like that. Kids often try drugs when they are offered them if they don't know better. They might believe their "friends" who tell them that the drugs are safe. They might even think that alcohol is safe. It's important to get our information about drugs and alcohol from a trusted adult. Drugs and alcohol are ALWAYS dangerous for kids to take. Most kids don't know all of the right information about drugs and alcohol to make good decisions.

Instruction – Input and Modeling: Discuss credible sources of information and why they are credible. Write these on the board so students have a visual.

Check for Understanding: Ask students whether their friends are a credible source of information. Ask whether parents are a good source of information. Choral responses are appropriate.

Guided Practice: You can use the following chart to organize the information. Provide a handout to each student.

People I can trust to know the right information:	Why I can trust these people:
Parents	They know a lot and care a lot about me.
Teachers	They have good information about drugs and alcohol, and they care a lot about me.
Counselors	They see a lot of kids who use drugs and alcohol, and they care about me.
Doctors	They know the effects of drugs, and they care about me.

Independent Practice: Students will complete their own chart independently with specific people in mind.

People I can trust to know the right information:	Why I can trust these people:

Activities:

1) Write a story about a kid who goes on a camping trip and encounters a mysterious plant growing in the woods. You decide whether the character makes a safe choice or an unsafe choice. Be sure to tell which your character chooses. Also include the consequences (good or bad) of his or her choice.

2) In a group of four or more students, pretend that you have found a bottle of household cleaner. You were cleaning the house for your mom. She said that if you don't finish the chore, you won't get to go to a birthday party you want to go to. She's at the store, and your older sister is babysitting. Decide as a group what you should do with the bottle, who you should tell, and whether you should finish cleaning with the mysterious cleaner.

3) Write a letter to one of the adults you chose in lesson 2. In your letter, include any questions you have about drugs, alcohol, or peer pressure. Make sure you tell the person you chose why you chose him or her.

Red Ribbon Week Lesson Plans

Grades 4–6

Lesson Plan: Why Do People Think Drugs and Alcohol Are So Great, Anyway?

This lesson should require approximately 30 minutes for instruction and practice. Extension activities might require more time or can be kept on hand for early finishers.

Objective: Students will demonstrate understanding of the ways alcohol, tobacco, and other drugs are marketed and advertised and that these have an impact upon substance use.

Content Standard: *Examine advertising strategies used for alcohol, tobacco, and other drugs.*

Method and Materials: Discussion, cut-and-paste poster project. Magazines, poster paper, scissors, glue.

Review: Read the following questions to the class and allow them to briefly discuss among themselves:

1) What are some commercials you have seen for beer?

2) When do these commercials typically come on TV?

3) Where do you see advertisements for cigarettes?

4) Has anyone ever noticed the people in the ads for smoking or drinking alcohol? Are they attractive and cool, or are they dull and average?

Anticipatory Set: Read the following story to the class.

Daniel's Disappointment

Daniel loved playing basketball more than almost anything else in the whole world. He loved watching basketball, too. Daniel and his dad would watch his favorite team and cheer during the whole game. Daniel often imagined during his games that he was on TV like his favorite professional players. He wished he could slam dunk a ball like the guys on TV. Even though he practiced every day after finishing his homework, Daniel couldn't even come close to dunking the basketball.

One day while Daniel and his father were watching a game on TV, a commercial came on for basketball shoes. Daniel's favorite player came on the screen and told the whole world his secret to his slam dunk! It was his SHOES! Daniel jumped up and down.

"Dad! Dad, I have to get those shoes so I can dunk!" Daniel knew his father would understand. The commercial guaranteed that he would be able to dunk if he just bought a pair of those special shoes!

"Daniel, the commercial is wrong. There is no shoe out there that can make a regular kid dunk like a pro basketball player. Otherwise, everyone who could afford those shoes would be a professional player," his father said.

Daniel remained convinced that the shoes were the missing link between him and his slam dunk. He was determined to buy those shoes. The next day, Daniel carefully counted the money in his piggy bank. He was still $20 short despite all of the tooth money, birthday money, and allowance he had saved over the years.

Daniel decided to mow lawns for the rest of the money. He needed to mow four lawns in order to earn the $20. Within a week, he had reached his goal. He couldn't wait to buy those special shoes and finally learn to slam dunk! Even though he disagreed with Daniel's decision, his dad let him make the purchase. Daniel was elated when he got home and stood before the basketball hoop above the garage. His new shoes were laced into place. Daniel took a deep breath and prepared to soar to the rim. He jumped – and – and – nothing. Nada. Zip, zilch, zero dunking. Daniel was crestfallen! He couldn't believe he had been wrong about the commercial! His father had been right. Now he had spent all of his hard-earned and even harder-saved money on a stupid pair of shoes that didn't help him dunk! In his disappointment, Daniel realized that he should have listened to his dad instead of the empty promises of the TV.

Introduction: Lead the class in a brief discussion with the following topic:

Advertisements can definitely be misleading. The only way many of them do lead is straight to disappointment. Yet they are very effective. What do you think some commercials and advertisements promise people that the product they are selling will do for them?

- Write student answers on the classroom whiteboard. Emphasize answers that are similar to the promises made by drugs and alcohol. (They will make you more popular, cool, perform better, etc.)

Instruction – Input and Modeling: Discuss with students the ways that alcohol and tobacco are presented to the public. Compare the advertisements they have seen with facts about the dangers of tobacco and alcohol that have been taught during Red Ribbon Week. Allow students to come to conclusions about whether the ads are misleading.

Check for Understanding: Ask students to locate an ad for their poster and hold up their magazine. Scan the room and make sure students are on target.

Guided Practice: Select two students to share their first chosen ads to bring to the front of the class. Allow them to use the whiteboard to write their first anti-ad for tobacco and alcohol along with their picture. Once students have seen this demonstrated, they can begin working on their own poster.

Independent Practice: Pass out magazines. Instruct students to create a collage of alcohol and tobacco ads found in the magazines. They are to cut out the pictures and paste them onto poster paper. Using markers, they will write anti-ads to tell the truth about smoking and drinking alcohol from facts they have learned during Red Ribbon Week.

Lesson Plan: Reactions Can Be Different

This lesson should require approximately 30 minutes for instruction and practice. Extension activities might require more time or can be kept on hand for early finishers.

Objective: Students will demonstrate an understanding that different people have different reactions to drugs and alcohol.

Content Standard: *Explain why individual reactions to alcohol and drug use may vary.*

Method and Materials: Demonstration, discussion, art project. Bowls and protective covering, vinegar, baking soda, and water as well as butcher paper and markers for *Uniquely Me* activity.

Review: Discuss the effects of drugs and alcohol that have been discussed throughout the week. Complete a KWL chart on the whiteboard to determine what students know about drug and alcohol reactions, what they want to know, and what they will learn about drugs and alcohol and their effects on the body.

Anticipatory Set: Ask students the following questions. Write their answers on the board and allow brief discussion among students.

1) Does anyone have any allergies?

2) What happens to a person who is allergic to peanuts who eats them?

3) What if you are not allergic to peanuts and you eat them?

4) Does everyone like the taste of peanut butter? (Take a poll.)

5) Why do we have different flavors of peanut butter (crunchy vs. creamy)?

Introduction: Discuss the ways that chemicals interact differently with one another, just as people react differently to peanuts. Demonstrate by adding a cup of vinegar to a cup of water and watch the reaction. Then add a cup of vinegar to a cup of baking soda and watch the reaction. Discuss the differences in the ways the three substances interacted.

Instruction – Input and Modeling: Discuss with the class the differences in human bodies. Weight, allergies, and tolerances all make a difference in how a person will react to a chemical substance such as drugs or alcohol. Use the example of Shaquille O'Neal and a kindergarten student. Would they be able to eat the same amount of pizza? Would they take the same amount of cough medicine for a cold? Who would need to drink more water every day?

Check for Understanding: Ask students a few questions to determine whether they are on target. Does everyone have the same basic response to food and chemicals? Do some people react differently to different chemicals or foods?

Guided Practice: Show students how to help one another make a *Uniquely Me* project by having one student lie down on the butcher paper while another student traces his or her outline. Then cut out the student's outline and proceed with the activity. (Use a premade sample to save time.) Students can decorate their cutout with positive drawings and messages about why they are unique individuals.

Independent Practice: Students will complete their Uniquely Me activity. If they finish early, they can complete a journal entry about what they have learned from today's lesson. Hang student projects in the classroom for the duration of Red Ribbon Week.

Activities:

1) Students will break into groups of four and create a newspaper page about the dangers of drugs and alcohol. They can include anti-advertisements and must include at least four articles on these dangers using facts learned during Red Ribbon Week.

2) Students will write a letter to either a tobacco company or an alcohol company asking them to remove advertisements that promise false things about their products. Using information learned during Red Ribbon Week lessons, they can present facts and statistics to back up their opinions.

3) Students will create a classroom mural stating individual reasons to say no to drugs and alcohol. Combining the information learned in previous lessons, students will express their desire to stay drug-free and unique.

Red Ribbon Week Anti-Drug Word Search

O	E	B	O	T	E	H	T	R	X
N	E	C	O	C	R	Z	H	Y	Z
W	J	N	I	D	O	H	F	H	D
Q	P	O	I	X	Y	A	Z	T	T
N	H	L	O	C	M	R	D	L	H
C	G	A	A	N	I	M	I	A	V
V	X	Y	T	W	H	D	H	E	P
B	Y	D	R	U	G	S	E	H	B
N	U	J	D	E	J	M	R	M	O
Q	O	A	S	R	C	N	D	B	J

body   choice   drugs
harm   healthy   medicine

Red Ribbon Week Anti-Drug Word Search

K	O	S	K	Y	X	Y	D	Y	V	E	T	Z	Z	Q
E	S	U	P	F	W	N	D	W	L	O	S	L	M	F
L	O	H	O	C	L	A	L	B	B	G	H	W	B	C
E	L	R	T	C	M	M	I	A	U	Q	I	A	T	R
K	M	I	S	D	Z	S	C	R	G	N	C	W	R	R
M	I	F	Q	X	N	C	D	P	E	E	H	G	Y	M
Z	V	B	R	O	O	E	T	X	O	Z	L	L	H	J
H	T	R	P	A	I	C	A	U	B	B	C	L	I	L
Q	E	S	M	E	D	I	C	I	N	E	X	S	I	N
L	E	A	K	O	P	O	W	C	V	E	D	M	P	H
R	S	N	L	S	M	H	L	Q	T	R	N	O	I	B
K	C	E	Z	T	H	C	O	S	X	J	B	K	H	E
B	O	D	Y	X	H	V	B	Y	Q	T	C	I	M	C
G	B	O	J	I	T	Y	D	T	U	J	J	N	G	D
N	T	O	Y	A	Q	A	I	L	W	L	D	G	D	T

alcohol	beer	body	choice
drugs	harm	healthy	illegal
medicine	smoking	tobacco	wine

Red Ribbon Week Anti-Drug Word Search

E	X	E	R	C	I	S	E	D	G	K	Q	L	R	A	E	G	T	G	T
Z	S	E	Q	M	N	K	R	B	S	D	Y	E	A	N	T	O	P	J	C
Y	N	X	Y	X	A	U	R	U	N	E	S	D	I	G	B	P	R	Y	E
P	Z	W	F	T	G	S	I	E	P	P	T	C	O	A	E	C	N	C	P
L	N	L	S	S	K	M	Z	N	O	X	I	T	C	B	X	L	W	A	S
E	O	I	C	I	R	O	M	N	N	D	P	C	E	N	G	T	L	T	E
D	M	W	A	F	F	K	S	A	E	I	O	J	R	R	O	T	A	I	R
G	X	N	M	F	J	I	G	M	I	W	Z	U	E	P	A	J	U	Z	O
E	H	W	H	G	B	N	U	A	E	U	T	N	T	M	Q	G	V	Q	F
X	F	D	W	I	M	G	W	I	N	E	Y	P	C	R	F	T	I	M	L
D	K	Y	L	W	L	V	W	Z	S	Q	B	Z	A	A	O	R	V	C	I
S	S	I	E	L	B	I	S	N	O	P	S	E	R	H	M	G	E	G	J
H	T	Z	T	K	T	B	B	X	W	S	F	H	A	M	V	I	R	E	D
Y	E	I	O	I	L	O	H	O	C	L	A	N	H	K	X	P	X	G	U
B	Q	A	U	D	E	V	U	P	U	H	C	G	C	E	V	A	R	B	E
H	L	Z	L	G	R	Y	Z	Y	S	M	O	N	B	N	X	Y	A	A	N
A	G	H	C	T	C	O	U	R	A	G	E	I	H	N	H	V	B	S	R
T	S	D	T	F	H	A	I	T	N	J	X	P	C	K	M	H	O	E	M
T	D	E	G	T	P	Y	R	N	B	U	E	B	H	E	O	P	E	Q	M
R	M	V	R	U	F	T	T	E	N	O	K	L	F	F	P	B	O	Z	W

alcohol	beer	body	brave	character
choice	cigarettes	courage	drugs	free
harm	healthy	illegal	medicine	mistake
pledge	respect	smoking	tobacco	wine

BONUS: What's one thing you can do instead of smoking or drinking?

BONUS: When you decide not to smoke or drink, you are being_____.

BONUS: It is your_____to stay drug free.

Resources and Websites

1. http://www.imdrugfree.com/ Prevention Partners can help you plan your Red Ribbon Week celebration with our Red Ribbon Week activities and classroom exercises.

2. http://www.preventionpartners.com/shop/browse_catalog.cfm?campaign=D &s=dom&t=804Products for Red Ribbon Week success

3. http://www.nfp.org/default.asp?PageNum=617 Facts about Red Ribbon Week

4. http://redribbon.org/ Resources for national event and local school planning

5. http://www.redribboncoalition.com/ Procedures and guidelines for RRW coordinators and sites

6. http://www.redribbonresources.com/ Products, services, and planning resources for RRW

7. http://www.elks.org/dap/redRibbonWeek.cfm History and fact sheets for RRW

8. http://www.justice.gov/dea/redribbon/RedRibbonCampaign.shtml The official place for RRW supporters and observers

9. http://www.toosmarttostart.samhsa.gov/Start.aspx Interactive site with games and information

10. http://www.abovetheinfluence.com/ Interactive site for children, teens, and parents about drugs and alcohol

11. http://www.stopalcoholabuse.gov/RedRibbonWeek/ Resources for facts, activities, and information about RRW history

12. http://bblocks.samhsa.gov/ Partnership site for families and educators to keep kids aware and off drugs

13. http://girlshealth.gov/ General resources specifically for girls about drugs

14. http://www.dare-america.com/kids/index_3.htm Interactive site for kids and parents by law enforcement with drug facts and information

15. http://mediasmarts.ca/ Media awareness for kids about drugs and alcohol

16. http://www.redribbonmonth.org/ Resource site for activities, organizations, and promotion of extending RRW

17. http://www.methproject.org/ Information about meth and its effects (for older kids)

18. http://www.thecoolspot.gov/ Interactive site for kids to get information about the dangers of drugs

19. http://science.education.nih.gov/supplements/nih3/alcohol/default.htm Resource for older kids about the effects of alcohol on the human body

20. http://www.teens.drugabuse.gov/ Facts for teens and kids about drug dangers, peer pressure, and other related topics

21. http://www.drugabuse.gov/publications/marijuana-facts-teens Facts about marijuana for teens and kids

22. http://www.drugs.indiana.edu/ Discussions about disease prevention related to drug use

23. http://www.justice.gov/dea/redribbon/Toolkit_Page/Red-Ribbon-Fact-Sheet.pdfActivities and updates for RRW

24. Local Police Department: Will usually come out and do a demonstration for RRW upon request

25. Local Fire Department: Will usually come out and do a demonstration for RRW upon request

CHARLIE AND THE CURIOUS CLUB...CANDY OR MEDICINE?
By Erainna Winnett, EdS.

Charlie is curious about everything. He and his best friend, Dillin, are part of the Curious Club. Their curiosity is peaked when Ms. Shirley and her pet parrot, Pierre, move in next door. When they see a colorful trinket filled with that they think is candy, the Curious Club discovers being curious is a good thing, but curiosity without caution can be dangerous.

Join Charlie, Dillin and Pierre as together they learn about the dangers of mistaking medicine for candy.

Topic: Curiosity and Decision Making

Grades: PK-2

Pages: 32

Size: 8 x 10

Binding: Softcover

Price: $10.95

Recommended: Class Read Aloud

View book trailer, PowerPoint template and print FREE activity pages at Celebratingredribbonweek.com

SARAH'S SICK DAY by Erainna Winnett, EdS.

Sarah really wants to go to school today, but she's feeling very sick. It's share day, her favorite day of the week. If she stays home, she'll miss sharing her new birthday doll, she'll miss snack time with her friend, Grace, and she'll miss story time. Her mom says she's going to call the doctor, but Sarah knows just what medicine she should take to feel better—or does she?

Topic: Decision Making

Grades: PK-2

Pages: 32

Size: 8.5 x 8.5

Binding: Softcover

Price: $10.95

Recommended: Class Read Aloud

View book trailer, PowerPoint template and print FREE activity pages at Celebratingredribbonweek.com

NO THANKS! SAYING NO TO ALCOHOL AND DRUGS
By Erainna Winnett, EdS.

It's hard to know what to say when older kids pressure you to do something you know is wrong. Blake is a fifth-grader with one thing on his mind: karate. He needs his friend's older brother, Jacob, to help him get ready for a big karate tournament. But Jacob's new friend, Ryan, has other ideas—that could get all of them into a lot of trouble. What will Blake decide when the right thing to do is also the hardest thing to do?

Topic: Drug and Alcohol Peer Pressure

Grades: 3-6

Pages: 32

Size: 8 x 10

Binding: Softcover

Price: $10.95

Recommended: Class Read Aloud

View book trailer, PowerPoint template and print FREE activity pages at Celebratingredribbonweek.com

Made in the USA
Lexington, KY
16 August 2017